My Church Smells Like Popcorn

My Church Smells Like Popcorn

Themes of Christian Faith in 21st Century Movies

Drew Kirtley

ISBN: 978-0-359-33538-1

ISBN 978-0-359-33538-1

90000

9 780359 335381

For Meghan, Keely, and Kennedy

&

to the memory
of my friend and mentor,
Ryan Benton

Contents

Foreword

The melody comes from the back of the room. It is a song of pain, a plea for help. The graduate students meditate on the message; some scribble obscure notes. In this moment, all is silent but the music and the sound of pens on notepads. It makes me wonder what people are going through beneath the surface, what the journal entries are really about. The harmonies continue as a few more students trickle into the room from the outside world, and I get the feeling this is their escape from the monotony (at least the heat) for a brief moment as they wander in and find a seat. They bring their troubles in and probably sling them back over a shoulder before they leave, in some unknown bag designed just for that, but in here, in the cool, everyone seems content as they sit at the table, in the moment, amongst all the others with mortgages and eight-year-olds.

It's November 2010, and I sit in the back row of a small room at Phillips Theological Seminary in Tulsa, Oklahoma, a room that smells like new carpet, on what is the last day of the semester, the day grades are to be posted. Today the students are discussing self-care and how, as pastors, they will effectively deal with some of the most difficult issues they will face. The kid next to me begins to read from his essay—I call him a kid in relation to the other students in the class—and he inspires me from the start. He writes well on themes of hope and redemption and speaks of hope as the "ultimate healing mechanism." It is clear to me that his hope will light the way for many who will find themselves in a struggle in life.

I have never attended Phillips Seminary. I had been a guest that day of the kid sitting next to me, the kid sweating bullets for the posting of the grades later that afternoon, the eventual author of this book, and although his report card, so to speak, would turn out fine, he had to exercise no small amount of faith that day, as I remember it. Even then, one thing was clear to me: grades are not the most important things in this world, and regardless of how it all turned out, he would still do beautiful things for people, as he already had for me on so many occasions.

While the class elders rambled on about how a pastor should be and think and feel, Drew added his own two cents when he had the opportunity, the wisdom he had obviously so acutely acquired. His ideas were somehow different than the rest, and I experienced something of a paradigm shift every time he spoke. It wasn't that the others didn't care about people; it was just that most of their talk seemed to be drawing from a chapter in a book somewhere far-off, and my friend answered as if he were caring for a brother or a sister. True love, after all, knows nothing of theory.

Drew, whom I have known for so long now, I have always known to communicate from his heart. It is his example (out-going and open to everyone) that has always challenged me, and I am fortunate to call him my friend, as much now as ever. Through this book, I have no doubt you will meet the man I've been talking about, and if you already know him, in reading it, I have no doubt it will be like meeting him all over again. His words, as always, are poignant, and they flow forth from a wellspring of love and well meaning.

Now, regarding his passion for movies… Since we met on that small college campus over a decade ago, movies have provided something like the bedrock of our friendship. We have seen countless films together over the years—even when we were the only ones in the sweltering theater on a slow Tuesday night— and we've had conversations about many more than that. Through these conversations, I've learned a lot about life, about love, and about what it means to find God in the world. His observations have always provided for me a new way of looking at things, including my own life and circumstances, and they have always left me a little better than I was in the opening credits. I know this book will do the same for you.

- Matt F. Parcher

Introduction

A few days before my birthday, my wife was sitting across the room, ordering my present on her phone. She didn't care if I knew what I was getting and I wasn't patient enough to wait until the following Sunday.

"Do you want to go to the 2:45 or 6:00 showing?" she asked.

We were going to the movies because she knows that's my favorite thing to do, and with a 3-year-old daughter, it's not very often we get out of the house at all.

We decided on the 2:45 p.m. showtime and paid a little extra for tickets to the theater with reclining seats. It's all about the experience, after all.

Then, before entering her credit card number, she let out an irritated sigh.

"Is the 5th row from the back, 7th row from the front OK?"

I hesitated.

"Here, you just pick the seats because you're the one who's picky about it," she replied.

I excitedly reached for the phone and moved our seats a row closer to the front and just a hair closer to the middle.

Normally, she wouldn't have bothered asking, but it *was* my birthday present. I handed back the phone and smirked as she rolled her eyes and ordered the tickets.

I know I should've just been thankful for the gift, but if given the opportunity to improve a movie-going experience (even by a row), I can't help myself.

Going to the movies has always been one of my favorite hobbies, but as I get older it has become something much more.

It has become nothing shy of a religious experience for me.

And the theater has become like a church.

I should explain.

As a Christian, and even more so as a minister, part of my calling is to be a storyteller.

Jesus of Nazareth called his followers to be witnesses, to tell stories about their experiences, and to spread his Good News to all the nations. And his Good News came in the form of stories.

When Jesus needed to get his point across about forgiveness, he told a radical story about a father and son.

When he wanted to change the hearts and minds of people regarding their enemies, he told a story of a Samaritan man who broke the "social rules" in order to love his enemy.

And every now and then, Jesus created his own story, one that would be told for years to come.

He got people to tell the story about that one time he approached a woman at a well and engaged in conversation with her.

He would touch people who were considered "unclean" and not to be touched.

And people talked about it.

People spread the word.

People told that story.

Then, he did the unthinkable.

The carpenter from Nazareth, a place from which no good could possibly come, forgave the very people who nailed him to a cross, mocked him, spat on him, and stood by idly as he was killed.

And people still tell that story.

Some say it's the greatest ever told.

But don't let that intimidate you. Your story is important too. The ways you've experienced the Holy Spirit are part of the ongoing story of God. And the stories we tell each other can shine a light on ways God has been revealed in our time. They can open people's ears and eyes to ways people might not expect to encounter the Good News of Christ.

The stories in our culture are told in a variety of ways, but perhaps none more popular, or widely spread than on that big, silver screen with the smell of popcorn in the air.

That is where I see and hear new stories from God, sometimes more than anywhere else.

Yeah, sometimes it's a curse.

I can hardly watch a movie anymore without thinking about how it could influence a sermon or a Bible lesson for the youth group.

But once I leave the theater, the good stories stay with me.

And the more stories I hear, the more I must admit: There are no authentic stories that are "bad" stories.

A good friend once told me, "I will forgive any shortcomings a film has if the thing has heart."

I think that's true for all stories, but especially movies.

They make an impression somewhere on me, and whether it's a year later or the very next day, part of a story makes its way into my faith life. They influence the way I think about God's role in the world, in the church, and in my personal life.

And once I accepted it, the theater became a place I went to seek a word from God.

I believe God speaks to different people in many different ways, and so my hope with this book is for one of two things.

I hope the stories I've heard, in the movies I've seen, will provide a new insight for you into the Good News of Christ.

Or I hope that through reading about the ways I've experienced God's story in movies, you might begin to notice the unique and unusual places the Holy is revealed to you.

Either way, I hope you enjoy this collection that is just a fraction of the movies from which I've gained a new insight or new perspective on Christ's message.

And for the full experience, read this book with a bucket of popcorn and an ice-cold pop.

My Church Smells Like Popcorn

Part I: Blockbusters

NOAH (2014)

"We have been entrusted with a task much greater than our own desires."

- Noah

In the beginning God created the heavens and the earth.
Now the earth was formless and empty, darkness was over
the surface of the deep, and the Spirit of God was
hovering over the waters.

And God said, "Let there be light," and there was light. God
saw that the light was good, and he separated the light from
the darkness. God called the light "day," and the darkness he
called "night." And there was evening, and there was
morning—the first day.

- Genesis 1:1-5

I want to address one small detail before we get started.

This book is about my experience finding inspiration from a place that most would not consider religious, other than when the occasional "Christian movie" is playing around the Christmas or Easter season.

However, I would argue that some of the best stories Jesus told, as well as some of the most influential stories of our time, are not necessarily told through a "Christian lens", but through the eyes and ears of someone just simply paying attention to the world.

That's exactly what makes director, Darren Aronofsky's epic biblical drama, *Noah*, the perfect movie with which to begin.

When this movie was released in theaters, I was initially thrilled.

Finally, a talented, accomplished director and actor (Russell Crowe as Noah) were going to tackle one of the greatest, most well known stories from the Bible. What could go wrong?

Then the reviews came pouring in.

Except it wasn't reviews from movie critics that caught me off-guard, but rather from "church" people themselves. I was completely overwhelmed as a minster by the number of people who felt the need to explain every way in which this movie "strayed from the scriptures."

"It's just not true to the story."

"Hollywood is taking liberties with the scripture."

"This is *not* a Christian movie about Noah."

"Stay away from this false teaching!"

I'm not exaggerating. Those were things I heard.

But here's the funny thing. I went into this movie with a group of students, who collectively came out with more interest in reading about Noah than when they entered the theater. And not only that, but I personally had a newfound awareness in the concept of creation and God as a Creator.

That's what this movie is about.

Throughout the film, Noah constantly refers to God as "Creator" while the theme returns repeatedly to the importance of the environment and acknowledging the value in all of God's creations.

Some might say that the filmmakers did not want to *acknowledge* God so they simply decided to call God by the name, "Creator," instead.

Really?

I don't find myself offended when someone calls me "Pastor" or "Reverend" or even "pal" or "brother" occasionally.

What happened to the phrase "I am" being something that evoked imagination and wonder at the idea of God being fully present in all places and in all things?

In fact, wouldn't calling God something like "Creator" acknowledge the belief that God *did* in fact create the world and everything in it?

That sounds to me like giving credit where credit is due.

That sounds like a Christian message.

Now, does this mean that the movie *Noah* should replace the story in scripture altogether? I don't think so. But if we weren't allowed to use our imaginations when reading scripture and think about the things God has been involved in outside of the words in the Bible, then we are limiting what our minds think is possible for God and those who seek to make God's will on Earth as it is in Heaven.

So, where do we go from here?

I started this chapter explaining how I was inspired and challenged in my faith by the movie *Noah,* and now I want to look at others like it.

Movies have consistently been one of, if not *the* primary source of inspiration for me over the years, and I have come to realize that in my experience, finding the Word of God in a movie is far from unusual.

Often, we hear folks talk about where God couldn't *possibly* be found.

But I would ask, "Wouldn't that be exactly where God needed to be the most?"

If God were only revealed through scriptures in the Bible and on Sunday mornings at 10:30, then wouldn't it be awfully hard to reach others with the message of Jesus?

And that's where we go from here.

In the following pages, I've included the some of the unlikeliest of ways, in the unlikeliest of movies, that I have encountered the Word of God.

I've found sermon inspiration while sitting by myself in a movie theater, watching a movie nobody else wanted to see. I have taken notes in my phone while watching a cheesy romantic comedy with my wife, or a superhero comic-book movie with my friends. I have watched movies that wouldn't be shown in a church because they're "not Christian-based", and yet they gave me a glimpse of Jesus. I have quite literally found God when I was deliberately looking for something else.

Sometimes I have even just been looking for an escape, and yet that was the last thing I could do, because God has a way of finding us precisely where we are.

And I'm at the movies a lot.

So again, these are some more examples of how it has happened for me.

I hope it happens for you.

Star Wars: The Force Awakens (2015)

"I am no Jedi, but I know the Force. It moves through and surrounds every living thing. Close your eyes… Feel it… The light... it's always been there. It will guide you."

- Maz Kanata

Live by the Spirit, I say, and do not gratify the desires of the flesh. For what the flesh desires is opposed to the Spirit, and what the Spirit desires is opposed to the flesh; for these are opposed to each other, to prevent you from doing what you want. But if you are led by the Spirit, you are not subject to the law. Now the works of the flesh are obvious: fornication, impurity, licentiousness, idolatry, sorcery, enmities, strife, jealousy, anger, quarrels, dissensions, factions, envy, drunkenness, carousing, and things like these. I am warning you, as I warned you before: those who do such things will not inherit the kingdom of God.

By contrast, the fruit of the Spirit is love, joy, peace, patience, kindness, generosity, faithfulness, gentleness, and self-control. There is no law against such things. And those who belong to Christ Jesus have crucified the flesh with its passions and desires. If we live by the Spirit, let us also be guided by the Spirit.

- Galatians 5:16-25

If any movies have been a constant part of my life since childhood, they're the original *Star Wars* trilogy. Those movies have been at the pinnacle of entertainment in my life for twenty-plus years. So, when Disney acquired the rights to the franchise, it was like a flame that had been extinguished was lit once again. Those of you who can relate know that's not an exaggeration.

My dad and I saw *The Force Awakens* in the theater together.

It was nostalgic and awesome and everything in between.

But for me, and I'm sure millions of others, the best part of the movie was revisiting everyone's favorite smuggler, Han Solo.

Even if you're not a *Star Wars* person, this is a fascinating character.

Here's a guy who, in the original 1977 classic, *Star Wars: A New Hope,* lives in a world of unbelievable things including aliens, intergalactic space travel, lightsabers, and more. Yet the *one* thing he has trouble wrapping his mind around is the idea of the Force.

But of course, to the audience (especially the religious audience), the Force is a bit familiar. Obi-Wan Kenobi describes the Force as "an energy field created by all living things. It surrounds us, penetrates us, and binds the galaxy together."

Now, if that doesn't sound like God, or the Holy Spirit, then I don't know what does. There have probably been thousands of references to one kind of spiritual practice or another when people talk about the Force and its religious parallels.

So, when Han Solo mocks his newfound passengers by brushing off talk of the Force, we can't help but be reminded of those who criticize religion today.

"Hokey religions and ancient weapons are no match for a good blaster at your side, kid," he famously quipped.

It's such a familiar response.

Yet, I find it fascinating that this character, one who openly rejects the possibility of the Force being real, has one of the subtlest, yet most profound changes of heart thirty years later.

In a scene from *The Force Awakens,* we find out that Han has seen and experienced enough to admit the fact that the Force has become real to him. But it doesn't seem like he was merely talked into it.

It doesn't seem like he lost an argument.

Nobody *proved* it to him.

He has the look of someone who experienced the Force for himself.

So, what happened?

What was the secret to the all-powerful method of evangelism that made Han Solo a believer?

Well, we don't know. But we do get a hint later in the movie, and that hint speaks volumes about the way Christianity, just like the Force, has been distorted over time.

The group is about to sneak into a heavily guarded building when they realize they're chances of success are slim-to-none. (Never tell Han Solo the odds.)

Finn, one of the newest *Star Wars* characters, proclaims, "We'll use the Force!"

Here is where this all connects.

Imagine a time when you were searching for something.

Maybe you're seeking an answer at a confusing time in life.

Maybe you're questioning the nature of God after the loss of a loved one.

Maybe you're facing a difficult trial yourself.

Can't you hear someone saying to you, "Just pray about it because God has an answer." Or how about, "If you have enough faith, it'll all work out." After all, doesn't the Bible say something about asking and you'll receive? Or seek and you will find?

Well, yes it does.

But just like in the movie, these are often just empty responses to fully loaded questions.

After Finn excitedly exclaims that the group should use the Force, he is met with a quick and funny, yet profoundly deep response from the once skeptical war hero.

"That's not how the Force works!" says Solo.

This not only serves as a moment of comedic relief before a series of emotional final scenes, but also gives the audience a glimpse into Han Solo's transformation from a skeptical nonbeliever into a wise, yet still skeptical, voice of reason.

He admits that the Force is real. Then he admits that it's also misunderstood.

This is a picture-perfect example of Christianity today.

In the *Star Wars* movies, we learn that the Jedi had spent hundreds and hundreds of years studying, training, and practicing the use of the Force.

Then, when a young, enthusiastic newcomer faces a difficult situation, he assumes that using the Force will obviously solve all his problems. And, why wouldn't it? "May the Force be with you" is perhaps the most recognizable phrases in the world. It's got to be *that easy*, right?

But the Force isn't a genie in a bottle.

Neither is Christianity.

So, if that *isn't* how the Force works, and this *isn't* how Christianity works, then where is the disconnect? What are we doing wrong? Let's shift gears and look at a story of Jesus to see if we can figure it out.

This is an example of a common misconception about Christianity and how God often gets mistaken for an easy, quick, problem solver, whose sole purpose is to make our lives better.

But once again, Jesus gets it right.

One of my favorite things that Jesus did was just breathe.

Take a moment.

Pause.

Here's this guy who had every disadvantage one could have in his time. He was a peasant, he didn't have money, and he was down and out.

He was essentially, in the eyes of society, the scum of the earth. And to make matters worse, for every person who liked him, there were probably two people who *didn't* like him.

He was also a rebel.

He proclaimed goodness and truth with authority. He stood up for outcasts, even if that meant standing against people of his own religion. And he did it all while loving God and loving his neighbor.

He had a hard life. But instead of panicking, he would simply carry out his task, collect himself, and breathe.

The question is: How could someone *breathe* when the iron fist of powerful people and powerful systems in the world was clinched around him, suffocating him, and casting him out.

The answer is simple.

Approval and acceptance were not his life source, like they are with so many of us, most of the time.

The clearest example of this way of life comes when Jesus was on a boat with his disciples in the middle of a storm. The disciples were panicked. Life around them was pure chaos. Their boat was being tossed around like a rag doll and they were afraid for their lives.

Meanwhile, Jesus breathed.

More specifically, he slept… on the boat.

Then when his disciples woke him up, Jesus' response was priceless. The disciples asked him, "Teacher, don't you care if we drown?"

"Don't you care...?"

That is the mindset that still drowns our faith today.

We have this automatic human response that tells us if we *care* about something, we should panic. If something is going wrong in our lives, we *need* to panic. We have to worry or we must not care.

Isn't that odd?

If someone happens to have the rare ability to be *calm* or have a presence of *peace* amid all the chaos in the world today, then it must be obvious that they clearly don't care enough about the situation. If they cared, they'd panic just like the rest of us. But something is wrong with this picture, and as usual Jesus gives us an alternative solution.

As the story goes in the Book of Mark, Chapter 4, verses 39-40,

He got up, rebuked the wind and said to the waves, "Quiet! Be still!" Then the wind died down and it was completely calm. He said to his disciples, "Why are you so afraid? Do you still have no faith?"

This is where the confusion happens.

We sometimes think that having faith means believing that God will solve all our problems. We assume that having faith means believing a situation will turn out better than it is.

We even go as far as to think that if life doesn't improve, then our faith just doesn't work in real life. So, then our faith becomes less real because its effectiveness starts to depends on the season.

If life is sunny, our faith is sunny, but if life feels like the cold of winter, then our faith might as well be frozen until spring.

This is where the meaning of faith has become diluted, but once again, Jesus shines a light on the confusion in this story.

Jesus calmed the storm when the disciples were wondering why their faith wasn't making the rain and wind cease. He revealed to his friends that this wasn't how faith worked.

When Jesus asked them if they *still* didn't have faith, he wasn't referring to their inability to stop the storm on their own. He asked why they were afraid in the midst of the storm. Why would they fear the weather if they had faith that God was there too?

Jesus' question reveals our answer.

Having faith in God doesn't mean that God will solve your problems. It means having faith that God is in your midst, *during* the problems.

It means believing that God will be God no matter what you're going through, good times or bad, highs or lows, storm or no storm.

See, the answer was in *Star Wars* all along.

23

It's revealed through a sort of blessing, or in the way the characters bid farewell to one another.

"May the Force be with you."

It's like they're saying that whatever happens, may you be in the presence of the Force. The energy that surrounds us, penetrates us, and binds us together. It almost sounds like being the presence of God.

When we approach the Christmas season, we might hear the song, "O Come, O Come Immanuel." Immanuel is a Hebrew word which means "God is with us."

Let that be your prayer today.

No matter what stage of life you're in, no matter how high or low you think you are, and no matter how bad the storm looks or feels around you… Let your prayer be that God is with you.

Because God brings peace. And patience. And goodness. And a lot of other things that tend to calm the storms.

That's what it means to have faith.

May God be with you, always.

X-Men: Days of Future Past (2014)

"Just because someone stumbles and loses their path, doesn't mean they're lost forever."

- Charles Xavier

I appeal to you therefore, brothers and sisters, by the mercies of God, to present your bodies as a living sacrifice, holy and acceptable to God, which is your spiritual worship. Do not be conformed to this world, but be transformed by the renewing of your minds, so that you may discern what is the will of God—what is good and acceptable and perfect.

- Romans 12:1-2

OBJECTS IN MIRROR ARE CLOSER THAN THEY APPEAR

We've all seen the little inscription on the passenger-side mirror of a vehicle, warning us that the motorcycle or semi-truck isn't as far behind us as we might have thought.

What a powerful metaphor for the past, right?

It's never as far away as we think it is.

The past is something we encounter all the time, meaning sometimes the past isn't quite *in the past* all the time, is it? Just like the vehicles in the little warning on the mirror, the past is something that creeps back up on us from time to time. Sometimes we must face it again and figure out how to deal with it.

The problem is that we often run into conflicting instructions on how exactly we should treat the past.

Sometimes we should "*learn* from the past."

Sometimes we should "stop *living* in the past."

Sometimes we should "let it go" because it's *already* in the past.

And often, life would be better if everything would just "go back to the way things were before."

So, how *are* we supposed to deal with the past? We know it's there. Some people think about it all the time, wishing they could go back. Some spend all their time trying to forget about it.

Either way, it takes some effort to turn around and confront it. And the further we come into the present, the more there is of the past.

It is looming and growing by the second.

That's why I think those little words on the side mirrors are helpful in more ways than one.

Just like when driving a car, simply because something is out of sight doesn't mean that it's behind you. And trying to act like it is could cause a crash.

If something in still on our mind, it's not in the past, but in the present.

If something from the past is impacting the way we live on a day-to-day basis, that issue is *presently* there. The past molds us, shapes us, and makes us who we are in the present.

So, once we realize that these "objects" are close to us, then what happens?

Well, it's far less scary if it's not really chasing us, right?

The past only chases us if we run from it.

Think of this on a much larger scale. As a county, we *need* our history. We insist that children learn history as a part of basic education from an early age. It's a requirement in almost any field of study. Most cultures have deemed it necessary for people to understand history.

So why is it that we run from our history on a personal level?

One could make the argument that it is just as important to know one's own history as well.

Of course, we can only study history, both national and personal history, from our own perspective, when in fact there are multiple perspectives. We can never really know the history of our own actions as told from every person we've encountered. So what's the answer?

This is where we get a choice regarding out past.

In the 2014 movie, *X-Men: Days of Future Past*, the "mutants" are facing extinction in a post-apocalyptic world. Mutants are basically humans who have evolved and now possess different special abilities. They are outcasts in society and are considered by many to be dangerous. Of course, this is a result of stereotyping and has led to an all-out war between humans and mutants.

Long story short, the X-Men (a team of mutants who believe in peace between humans and mutants), decide to send someone back in time to prevent the war from happening, which would restore peace in the world.

Professor Xavier, the leader of the X-Men, realizes that they can change the past as he begins to wonder about all the new possibilities for the future. This is when he says something that might help us change the way we think back about our own lives.

"The past: a new and uncertain world. A world of endless possibilities and infinite outcomes. Countless choices define our fate: each choice, each moment, a moment in the ripple of time. Enough ripple, and you change the tide... for the future is never truly set."

You are probably thinking, *"But we can't change the past."*

Well, you're right. We don't have time machines.

But can we not change the past?

I mean, if the object in the mirror is closer than it appears, what would happen if we reached out and grabbed it?

What would happen if we looked at it differently, from a different perspective?

What if we changed our minds about how we would interact with it?

If the past is going to linger around trying to haunt us, intimidate us, trying to keep us from moving forward, then there must be a way to fight back, right?

Professor X is right.

The past is a world of endless possibilities and infinite outcomes because we are the ones creating it.

We can look at certain parts of our past and become sad, angry, vengeful, or simply choose to remain living there, clinging onto things for the rest of our lives.

Or,

We can look at our past and decide *how* we are going to allow it to create the present. And by doing that, we are no longer running from the past, but creating it.

Here's an example.

The nemesis of the X-Men is a character called Magneto, one of the professor's oldest friends. He believes that peace is no longer achievable and tries to start a war between humans and mutants. At first glance, he is a purely evil man who wants nothing but destruction. He's the typical bad guy.

However, every now and then we are introduced to another piece of the puzzle to Magneto's past. His story begins to unravel for us to see the big picture. We start to learn about him, care about him, maybe even love him as much as we do the heroes in the story.

The audience reaches a point where, despite the amount of people he's killed, we feel sympathy for the guy.

From a distance, his past makes him appear to be one of the most dangerous, evil characters on screen. But as the past gets closer to us, as we get a better look at it, we begin to understand him. We get to know him.

As Christians, we are called to follow the example of Jesus of Nazareth.

Jesus had a technique when he was dealing with someone with a complicated past... he would get to know them.

That might sound simple but it's not.

By getting to know someone, Jesus was revealing that person's past and figuring out what events or decisions had contributed to the life they had created.

Jesus didn't try to find communities, but rather he helped create communities by helping people with complicated lives relate to one another.

He revealed their past to understand their present and give them a clear future.

So, the question for us remains the same.

What kind of life will we create?

As our respective pasts can tell us, progression isn't always a straight line, but a roller coaster ride full of unexpected twists and turns.

And our lives aren't just made up of the present, but the past and future as well.

How will you blend the three?

Will you run from the past? Will you live in it?

Will you look toward the future, ignoring the moment?

Or will you live in the present with a clear, helpful understanding of the past, and a bright, hopeful future.

The objects in the mirror might be closer than they appear, but one thing is certain…

The steering wheel is still in your hands.

The past: a new and uncertain world. A world of endless possibilities and infinite outcomes. Countless choices define our fate: each choice, each moment, a moment in the ripple of time. Enough ripple, and you change the tide… for the future is never truly set.

<u>THE DARK KNIGHT (2008)</u>

"Why should I hide who I am?"

- Harvey Dent

I am reminded of your sincere faith, a faith that lived first in your grandmother Lois and your mother Eunice and now, I am sure, lives in you. For this reason I remind you to rekindle the gift of God that is within you through the laying on of my hands; for God did not give us a spirit of cowardice, but rather a spirit of power and of love and of self-discipline.

- 2 Timothy 1:5-7

I remember the first time I told a friend of mine from high school that I was going into ministry.

We were sitting at my old high school gym watching a basketball game. She was telling me about how she would have to go through another year of college because she was changing her major. I told her I was finishing my undergrad program and taking a job as a youth minister.

She laughed and thought I was joking.

I can't blame her. It was actually pretty funny, given who I was in high school.

And if you would've told some of my friends from college, they would've just dismissed the idea altogether.

In fact, depending on which time in my life you go back to, you'll find not only a different opinion of me from others, but you might find a different me altogether.

I suppose this is true for all of us so some extent.

It's like there are six or seven Drews out there. And the question that gets people from both my past and present confused… Which Drew is the real one? Even scarier, do I know which one is real?

But make no mistake about it, who I am today is who I am. And if I've learned anything in my first decade in ministry, it's that I cannot afford for there to be more than one of me.

You see, the Christian faith has a struggle. It must deal with a hypocrisy label that will probably never go away. People say, "I'll never go to church because the church is full of hypocritical people." It's like people have a Sunday face and a Monday-Saturday face.

We all have different faces. Some of us many more than others.

The question is, how many faces do you have?

Do you act differently around different groups of friends?

Do you act differently around family?

Are you one person at school or work and another at church?

Are you one way to someone's face and another behind their back?

If so, you might be careful. The more faces you have, the harder it might be to really know yourself. And if you don't know yourself, it's nearly impossible for someone else to know you.

Here's an example:

The 2008 movie, *The Dark Knight*, is one of the best psychological thrillers of all time, in my opinion. It explores familiar characters, ones we've seen in movies for years, except it explores their minds, their thoughts, and their motives.

It's not just about Batman fighting the Joker, but rather it begs the question, *why* does he feel like he needs to fight the Joker.

It asks more questions too.

What makes these characters tick?

What do these characters really want?

Is Batman a good guy? Or can a person be truly good?

So many questions.

And to make these questions even more complicated, the movie introduces my favorite character, Harvey Dent, the Gotham City District Attorney who becomes the villain Two-Face.

Like a true psychological thriller, the movie doesn't label him bad, but instead asks the audience a question: Is this truly a bad guy? If so, why?

It dives into the life of this man and what makes him behave the way he does, make the choices he makes, and react the way he reacts.

Harvey is a man who put his life and the lives of his loved ones on the line for the greater good. And it took its toll on him. So, he makes a very real, human decision to get revenge on the people he blames for a tragedy.

It's a decision, which most, if not all of us would make.

And yet it's easy to sit in the theater and think, "That's the bad guy."

So, we root for Batman, just like we're told to do,

Just like we had already decided to do before we walked into the theater,

Just like we've always done.

But again, this movie isn't about good and evil. It's about good (represented by Batman), evil (represented by The Joker), and that space in between. That's where the Harvey Dent character comes into the picture. Two-Face is a wonderful resemblance of the duality of humankind.

Two sides, two personalities.

One is light, one is dark.

One appears attractive, the other scarred.

Two faces. One man.

Sound familiar?

See, the challenge with which this character presents the audience is to identify each side.

Which side is the *real* you?

Is it the side that appears flawless, warm, and happy?

Or is it the side that has been exposed? The side where the scars are visible and the soul of the person come through.

As Christians, we're pressured to wear our Sunday face, sometimes even when it's not Sunday. We think that because someone is a Christian, they're not allowed to have other faces anymore.

Because if you make a mistake, you're a hypocrite. You're what is wrong with Christianity today. But that's not true.

What's true is that Jesus was real.

And not just real in the sense that he existed, but in the sense that he was authentic. Jesus did things people considered *really* bad. And yet we call him perfect.

If you ask me, that's hypocritical.

I don't go to church because I'm perfect; I go because I'm not.

I don't work at a church to teach others to be like me, I try to teach others to be like Christ.

If you know me today, you know I don't wear a mask. I may have two faces, or three, or four, or five, but I wear them all the time.

Some might think it's weird to see a minister listening to non-Christian music, or swearing every now and then, or having a beer with dinner, or having tattoos, or whatever else a Christian isn't supposed to do.

But then, if I cover it up or hide it, I begin to mask those different faces. I'm a different Drew on Sunday than I am on Monday.

And yes, I'm always working to make the real Drew the best version I can, but not at the expense of keeping true to myself. That's the most important thing we can do as followers of Jesus to address the hypocrisy label. No more hiding.

So, I'll ask it again,

How many versions of you are there?

I want to challenge you.

Introduce people to yourself. People you already know. Maybe even to a version of you they haven't met yet.

The point is that practicing the Christian faith requires a real God and a real you.

Don't make the mistake of thinking there's a part of you God doesn't love.

And in turn, part of practicing Christianity is working on loving others the same way, unconditionally.

Loving people,

Not just certain versions of people. That's *conditional* love.

So, don't be a hypocrite.

Instead, be yourself.

(Unless you can be Batman.)

Part II: Based on a True Story

Walk the Line (2005)

"So y'all sit down, squat down or lie down but make yourselves at home because here's the one and only, Mr. Johnny Cash!"

-   June Carter

O Lord, you have searched me and known me.
You know when I sit down and when I rise up; you
discern my thoughts from far away.
You search out my path and my lying down, and are
acquainted with all my ways.
Even before a word is on my tongue, O Lord, you know it
completely.
You hem me in, behind and before, and lay your hand
upon me.
Such knowledge is too wonderful for me; it is so high that
I cannot attain it.

Where can I go from your spirit?
Or where can I flee from your presence?
If I ascend to heaven, you are there; if I make my bed in
Sheol, you are there.

If I take the wings of the morning and settle at the farthest
limits of the sea, even there your hand shall lead me, and
your right hand shall hold me fast.

If I say, "Surely the darkness shall cover me, and the light
around me become night," even the darkness is not dark
to you; the night is as bright as the day, for darkness is as
light to you.

For it was you who formed my inward parts; you knit me
together in my mother's womb.
I praise you, for I am fearfully and wonderfully made.
Wonderful are your works; that I know very well.
My frame was not hidden from you, when I was being
made in secret, intricately woven in the depths of the
earth.

- Psalm 139:1-15

What do you believe?

That is such a loaded question.

And to properly answer the question, we must first state out loud what is actually being asked. Are we asking what people actually believe in the depths of their heart, mind, and soul?

Are we asking what they *think* they believe?

Or are we asking what they *want* to believe?

Because those are three different things.

The movie, *Walk the Line*, takes us on a journey of a man who goes from one of these stages to the next until he finally figures out what he believes and why he believes it. And then we see how natural it becomes for him to finally "walk out" those beliefs.

As Christians, if we can figure out that process for ourselves, then we will be in good shape when it comes to following Jesus as authentically as we possibly can.

So, let's back up and start with the obvious... Johnny Cash is an icon.

And icons, for the most part, all have something in common:

They have figured out what makes them unique and they have maximized it to their full potential.

We rarely see an iconic figure trying to be like anyone else. In fact, its usually the quite the opposite. It is quite normal for people to try to imitate and follow those who have reached "iconic" status.

Every time there is a new basketball player who is considered the best, we begin hearing comparisons to Michael Jordan.

Every great golfer is the "next" Tiger Woods.

And anytime there is a wildly popular musician of one kind or another, they start getting mentioned in the same conversations as Elvis, The Beatles, or Johnny Cash.

Even Jesus went through this process!

People thought he was one of the prophets, while others thought he was John the Baptist.

Then Jesus asked a question all while creating his own identity in the world.

He asked, "Who do you say that I am?"

Jesus, as much of an understatement as it might seem to say, is an iconic figure in our culture.

Now, back to *Walk the Line*.

As an up-and-coming musician in the movie, Johnny Cash was struggling to find his niche, and after being brought up in a

Christian family (although the authenticity of that claim can be debated), Johnny and his band decided to become Gospel musicians.

So, while trying to audition for a record company, they begin playing a mundane, by the book, boring Gospel song.

After all, that's what they're supposed to do, right?

That's the niche to which they belong.

Just like as Christians, there are things we're "supposed" to do because that's what Christians do.

We look a certain way, talk a certain way, and most importantly, *believe* a certain way.

When I first got into ministry, I was the stereotypical youth pastor. You can look up hundreds of videos online to see what I mean by that.

I wanted to do everything I was supposed to do because that's the way I had seen it done. I wanted to be like every other pastor I had ever known, because if they were successful then why not just copy them?

But with music, as Johnny quickly learns the hard way, people can easily see through the front.

The man in charge of the record company shuts him down because he doesn't believe what Johnny is singing.

"You saying I don't believe in God?" Cash intensely responds.

Here is where our beliefs come into play.

It doesn't matter what we *say* we believe.

It doesn't matter what we *think* we believe.

It matters what we believe in our hearts, and whatever is in our hearts will always come out if we let it.

But letting it out means being vulnerable in using our own God-given voice to tell our own authentic story.

This is what we're called to do as disciples and followers of Jesus.

For Johnny Cash, that meant letting our years of anger, pain, frustration, and sadness.

And for the record label, as well as our listening pleasure, that meant something awesome, authentic, and beautiful:

It meant we got to hear the voice of a person whose heart had something to say.

The Psalmist was able to discover this level of honesty and acceptance with God. We read at the beginning of this chapter, familiar words in Psalm 139:1-15 that echo throughout history in the experiences of people who finally stumble upon this truth.

It would be easy to hear ego and arrogance in these words, but they are something much different.

These are freeing words.

These are the words of a person who has experienced the love of God in a way that has allowed them to love themselves for who God created them to be.

Jesus urged his followers to love God and to love their neighbor as themselves.

This is the love he was talking about.

Toward the end of the movie, Johnny is working with his company to make a live record while performing a concert at Folsom Prison.

The Johnny Cash in this scene is different Johnny Cash than we've witnessed throughout the movie. He stands tall in the office, wearing all black, sunglasses resting on his nose, and a cigarette in his mouth.

He is no longer concerned with the opinions of others when it comes to his identity and his music. He realizes his life story, his talent, and his own character are all part of what makes him special.

He is then able to turn that into ministry.

Johnny insists that he's playing a live concert in a prison because that is where he can make a difference in people's lives.

And if the record label isn't supportive, it doesn't matter.

What matters is that he loves himself, he recognizes his gift, and he can channel it in a way that will impact the world.

So, it's time to ask again…

What do you believe?

What do you believe about God, about being a Christian, and about yourself?

Once you figure that out, you will have started down a path of purpose.

There will never be another Johnny Cash and there will never stop being people who are trying to be the next Johnny Cash.

Which one will you be?

Will you spend your entire life trying to be something or someone else because you're supposed to?

Or will you be the most real, authentic version of yourself you can be?

That is what Christ calls us toward.

The worst thing we can demand is that all Christians become exactly the same person.

Christ's message was about loving yourself and the things that make you an individual, while at the same time loving others and helping them do the same.

You are fearfully and wonderfully made.

Believe that.

<u>Saving Mr. Banks (2013)</u>

"That's what we storytellers do. We restore order with imagination. We instill hope again and again and again."

- Walt Disney

Then the disciples came and asked him, "Why do you speak to them in parables?" He answered, "To you it has been given to know the secrets of the kingdom of heaven, but to them it has not been given. For to those who have, more will be given, and they will have an abundance; but from those who have nothing, even what they have will be taken away. The reason I speak to them in parables is that 'seeing they do not perceive, and hearing they do not listen, nor do they understand.' With them indeed is fulfilled the prophecy of Isaiah that says:

'You will indeed listen, but never understand,
 and you will indeed look, but never perceive.
For this people's heart has grown dull,
 and their ears are hard of hearing,
 and they have shut their eyes;
 so that they might not look with their eyes,
 and listen with their ears,
and understand with their heart and turn—
 and I would heal them.'
But blessed are your eyes, for they see, and your ears, for they hear. Truly I tell you, many prophets and righteous people longed to see what you see, but did not see it, and to hear what you hear, but did not hear it.

-   Matthew 13:10-17

What do you think Heaven is like?

That's a question I remember my dad asking when I was in a Sunday School class that he taught.

All the students had to get up in front of the class and draw on a big, blank sheet of paper, what we thought Heaven might look like.

There were people who went with the traditional assumptions of golden streets, big mansions for everyone, a big fence on the clouds with a line of people waiting to get in, and most importantly, God sitting on a throne with Jesus standing next to it.

Then came my friends' seemingly ridiculous additions to the image...

"I think there will be a lot of pizza," one of my friends said.

"That's what you eat when there's a lot of people to feed."

The funny thing is that made more sense to me than one thing in particular from the "traditional" Heaven drawing... the line outside the front gate.

A line? Really? Heaven is going to be no different from the popular slides at a water park? Or the biggest roller coaster at a theme park? We're going to be waiting for God knows how long?

That was the one thing I couldn't wrap my mind around. Of course, at that age I just accepted it and moved on. Maybe I would pass away during the non-busy hours or somehow earn a special pass to get in quicker.

Either way, I just decided to let it go and not get too bogged down with what Heaven was like, as long as I got in.

That is until I saw a certain movie, which changed my perception of Heaven and how I approach the subject.

The movie was *Saving Mr. Banks* starring Tom Hanks as Walt Disney.

It's the story of Mr. Disney attempting to purchase the film rights to the ever-popular *Mary Poppins* stories, written by Pamela "P.L." Travers.

You might not remember this movie having anything to do with heaven, and it doesn't, specifically. But it did act like a key to unlocking my understanding of heaven in the way Jesus helped people understand it.

Walt, as he liked to be called, has a nearly impossible time getting Ms. Travers to allow him to adapt her stories to film.

She didn't trust his vision, his word, and perhaps most importantly his imagination.

They never seemed to be on the same page in the way they imagined her beloved character, *Mary Poppins.*

Toward the end of the movie, Disney tells Travers that storytellers "restore order with imagination."

They "instill hope again and again and again." he reiterates.

I didn't know what he meant but it sounded great.

We restore order with imagination? Literally? How is that even possible?

I get the part about hope.

If you've made it this far through the book, then you already know about the power of hope that storytellers can have, specifically through movies. But "restoring order?" That seems like a stretch.

And then I stumbled upon a concept that tied it all together.

I took a seminary class in which we studied about Jesus from a historical perspective.

In fact, the main focus of the course was on the parables of Jesus.

Jesus the storyteller.

Wait a minute.

I had *just* watched this movie about a storyteller and there was this quote I had remembered about hope and restoring order.

Is there any way this was going to connect? I doubted it.

I was wrong.

In the class, we learned that for Jesus, the parables were a way of introducing people to the kingdom of heaven.

Jesus would tell a story about leavened bread or a treasure in a field. And in those stories, the audience didn't find a cheap lesson, but rather a brand new concept altogether.

These stories were Jesus' way of helping people to re-imagine the world.

First, imagine the world.

Our world.

Now, imagine a son who blows all the money his father gave him.

Then, imagine his father upon hearing this news.

Imagine his reaction.

Of course the audience would imagine anger, frustration, holding a grudge, even revenge.

But instead, Jesus asks his audience to re-imagine the world.

Re-imagine a new reaction from the father.

Imagine forgiveness.

That is what the kingdom of heaven is like.

The kingdom of heaven is like a lot of things according to Jesus.

The kingdom of heaven is like, well, imagine a Jewish traveler, who gets beaten and robbed and left along the side of the road.

Imagine all the reactions people would give him.

They'd probably be judging him, for starters.

How did he get there? He must be lazy.

Why doesn't he just go get a job?

I'm not giving him *my* hard-earned money, that's for sure.

They'd have all kinds of excuses.

Just *imagine* the excuses!

Now, imagine a priest walking by the Jewish traveler.

"Here comes the hero of the story," his audience would imagine.

But the priest just passes by...

Now imagine a Levite walking by the Jewish traveler.

"I can relate to him," imagines the listeners. "He must be the hero I'm picturing.

But the Levite doesn't stop, either.

Then, finally, a Samaritan sees the Jewish traveler on the side of the road.

"Oh boy…" The crowd can't *possibly imagine* this ending well for the poor, Jewish traveler.

After all, the Samaritan is his greatest enemy. What's he going to do, finish the job?

"Now…" Jesus must have thought to himself.

"Now I've got them imagining what the world wants them to imagine."

That's the moment in each of his parables when Jesus would flip the tables.

Pun intended.

Jesus challenges them yet again to re-imagine their world.

Re-imagine the ending to the story.

Imagine the enemy of the Jewish traveler not only going out of his way and helping him, but also going further.

Imagine him taking him to an inn and paying the innkeeper to *continue* taking care of the man.

His enemy.

His neighbor.

Re-imagine the world so that your enemies aren't your enemies.

Take everything, in fact, that this world makes you imagine… and hit the reset button.

So some of them did and some of them didn't.

And Jesus would tell story after story, parable after parable, asking and challenging people to have the courage to re-imagine the world in which they had gotten so comfortable.

If every person started doing that, just imagine what the world would be like after a while.

It would be a completely different, almost brand new world.

Hope would be instilled again and again and again.

Order would be restored through imagination.

Sully (2016)

"Everything is unprecedented until it happens for the first time."

- Captain Chelsey "Sully" Sullenberger

Again he entered the synagogue, and a man was there who had a withered hand. They watched him to see whether he would cure him on the Sabbath, so that they might accuse him. And he said to the man who had the withered hand, "Come forward." Then he said to them, "Is it lawful to do good or to do harm on the Sabbath, to save life or to kill?" But they were silent. He looked around at them with anger; he was grieved at their hardness of heart and said to the man, "Stretch out your hand." He stretched it out, and his hand was restored. The Pharisees went out and immediately conspired with the Herodians against him, how to destroy him.

- Mark 3:1-6

Truth.

Truth is a concept that is losing its luster these days.

Sometime around 2016, the term "fake news" became popular.

This, along with the rise in *actual* artificial stories and opinion-based content appearing across social media platforms, has injected a heavy dose of doubt into the world lately.

There has always been a certain level of doubt concerning Christianity and the legitimacy of the religion, the faith-based elements of scripture, and simply among Christians themselves when it comes to balancing the way of Jesus and facing trials and hardships in life.

However, truth is also a concept that, given time and a chance to speak, will rest its own case.

In other words, the truth shall set you free.

And perhaps nobody has learned that lesson in a more tense and scrutinized environment than Captain Chelsey "Sully" Sullenberger, as portrayed by Tom Hanks in the 2016 movie, *Sully.*

In the movie, Captain Sullenberger and First Officer Jeff Skiles are flying US Airways Flight 1549 from LaGuardia Airport in Queens, New York, to Charlotte Douglas International Airport in North Carolina, when a few minutes into the flight, the plane flew into a flock of birds and both engines were disabled.

After realizing they were without power and in all likelihood, unable to reach any nearby airports, Sully decided to attempt a highly unlikely water landing in the middle of the Hudson River, which runs straight through New York City.

After a "successful" landing, the crew and passengers evacuated without a single casualty. But while the public is quick to proclaim Sully as a hero, the incident leaves him shaken, questioning himself, and with reoccurring nightmares.

Then, in the midst of all his unwanted attention, Sully learns some complicated information about the details of the incident that basically suggest there was still a working engine, along with the National Transportation Safety Board's claim that several computerized simulations show the plane could have landed safely at a nearby airport. They suggest the accident may have been pilot error, which if true, would likely end Sully's career.

I remember when this happened in real-life and I remember when the movie was released.

What I didn't remember was any controversy surrounding the man who landed the plane in the Hudson River, although I do remember that is was a cool story and that he was considered a hero by many.

So, when I saw the trailer for the movie, I remember wondering what everyone was arguing about.

How could there even be a debate as to whether or not this man who saved all those lives did the right thing?

We forget sometimes that for there to be a hero, something has to have gone wrong at some point.

Nobody's life needs saved if nobody is in danger.

But in our society, which is more like Jesus' society than we realize sometimes, people talk about everything.

It's actually easier for us, logistically speaking, to talk to people about of anything and everything, than it ever has been for anyone in history.

We have the ability to put our thoughts, sometimes as soon as we have them, out into the world for everyone to read.

And we love to read them.

So, naturally, even if there's nothing wrong with a particular situation on the surface, people will try to dig until they find something wrong.

Why?

Because even when something *almost* goes wrong, someone tends to look bad as a result.

We want everything to be *someone's* fault.

So in the movie, even though every single person survived this plane crash, and even though it *wasn't even technically a crash,* the airline immediately had an image problem as a result of the information age.

And *that* is where the need for someone to blame comes into play.

They needed somewhere else for everyone to point their fingers.

But how could they possibly blame Sully?

He saved *everyone's* life aboard that plane.

He was instantly declared a hero.

There was only one thing they could do, and it's perhaps the most dangerous thing that is taking place in our world today.

They had to change people's perception of truth.

So, they introduced a question: What if Captain Sullenberger *wasn't* actually the hero?

What if they could've avoided the whole thing and landed safely back at the airport?

No movie would've been made, no book would've been written, and the airline would have saved face.

Everyone could just sweep this whole 'birds in the engine' thing under the rug and move on, right?

So they found a way out, or so they thought.

They found that the simulations showed evidence that Sully could've landed the plane safely.

The computers had proven it.

This, according to the Safety Board, was the "real truth".

Here is where both Jesus and Sully challenged the faith of those in authority. It starts with a question.

Have you ever broken a rule?

Better yet, have you ever broken a rule, but *in your mind*, it was the right thing to do?

Finally, have you ever broken a rule *because* of your *faith*?

In the Gospel of Matthew, we learn about this couple, Mary and Joseph.

Mary finds out that she is pregnant, before they even lived together, and that the Holy Spirit is responsible for the child. Joseph, scripture says, "being a righteous man" refused to expose Mary to public disgrace, and planned to dismiss her quietly.

Now, it doesn't go into any more details about Joseph "saving" Mary from public disgrace, but he helped to save her from a lot more than that.

A scripture from Leviticus, Chapter 20, verse 10 says, "If a man commits adultery with the wife of his neighbor, both the adulterer and the adulteress shall surely be put to death."

So, not only is Joseph showing mercy on Mary by keeping the whole thing quiet, he quite possibly helped to save her life.

How?

By breaking the rules of his "faith tradition".

Joseph, following the law of the Hebrew Scriptures, should be seeking to have Mary put to death.

But he feels a conflict between the scripture, or the rules, and the Holy Spirit.

This is an early example of one of the reasons we're given the Holy Spirit, and the reason is that our faith is a living, breathing thing, rather than just a book of rules.

It's fluid, not solid.

It's a way of life, not a planned out, structured practice.

And that's a hard concept for some people.

But Jesus, like he often does, comes along and simplifies things.

He intervenes when the Pharisees refuse to save the man with a withered hand.

He asks them which is lawful on the Sabbath, to save life or to kill?

This story of Jesus and his life of faith is similar the story of Captain Sullenberger and his heroic instincts.

People were looking for a reason to accuse Jesus of something.

Why?

Because Jesus was pushing the boundaries of their faith, as well as his *own* faith, and they needed to put a stop to it.

But they needed him to mess up.

They needed somewhere to point their fingers.

What they didn't plan on was his response.

He challenged them to remember the Sabbath.

Not the rules and the traditions surrounding the Sabbath.

He reminds them that it is a Holy day.

He reminds them that it is lawful to do *good*, rather than harm.

That's why we were given the Holy Spirit.

If we would practice living in the *spirit of Christ,* rather than simply trying to follow a set of rules, we would have a lot better chance of getting it right in the times when the birds hit the engine.

That's why the Holy Spirit *isn't* a book or a list of rules.

Does that mean we should throw away the Bible and just do whatever we want?

I wouldn't.

Jesus used the Holy Scriptures as a foundation for his faith, but he wasn't afraid to tell people they were using it in the wrong ways.

Because right and wrong isn't always black and white…

In the movie, Sully had trouble remembering what exactly happened in the cockpit until he listened to the playback.

He had trouble because he went into this "feeling" mode.

As a kid, his teacher told him, "Just fly the plane."

He relied on his instinct and training to react in the moment.

That's why as Christians we need both.

We need the old stories, the rules, the guidebook, and the foundation, but we also the Spirit for those times when something doesn't perfectly apply to a situation.

If we're living our faith the right way, then sometimes people will not agree with us. It won't look like how the world wants it to look.

A lot of times it's religious people who would come against us.

Sully tells his wife on the phone, before the final hearing, "I'll call you when they're done with me."

Because whether Sully was at the bar, out in public, or doing an interview with Letterman or Katie Couric, a lot of the public saw a hero, just like they saw in Jesus.

But the professionals and people who studied aviation saw a rule-breaker.

Just like the Pharisees, religious leaders, and teachers of the law saw Jesus.

But Sully, just like Jesus did, and just like we're called to do, had confidence in the truth.

And in the end, that is what set him free.

BlacKkKlansman (2018)

"If I'm not for myself, who will be?"

- Kwame Ture

When the Pharisees heard that he had silenced the Sadducees, they gathered together, and one of them, a lawyer, asked him a question to test him. "Teacher, which commandment in the law is the greatest?" He said to him, 'You shall love the Lord your God with all your heart, and with all your soul, and with all your mind.' This is the greatest and first commandment. And a second is like it: 'You shall love your neighbor as yourself.' On these two commandments hang all the law and the prophets."

- Matthew 22: 34-40

It has been said that young preachers should do theology with the Bible in one hand and the newspaper in the other.

In other words, it's impossible for a person of faith to study one without the other.

It's sometimes tempting to read scripture without paying attention to the news because the latter can be depressing.

It's also tempting to read the news and set the Bible aside, just assuming we know what we need to know already.

The task, as a follower of Christ, is to think about the world and practice our faith with both in mind.

This particular task, with that being said, can be a rather difficult one.

I was reminded of that as I walked out of a theater recently and had a quick, yet intimate moment with a fellow moviegoer.

I'll start by saying this is a delicate topic of discussion, and an even more delicate topic about which to write, especially in recent years.

The topic is racism.

I even questioned myself as to whether or not I wanted to address this particular issue after seeing this particular movie, because it didn't feel like mine to address.

But I couldn't ignore this one specific moment.

Let's start with the movie itself.

As a movie lover, I was immediately intrigued by the movie, *BlacKkKlansman*.

Here was a movie directed by the legendary Spike Lee, starring several of the most talented actors of this generation, including John David Washington, Laura Harrier, Adam Driver, and Topher Grace.

And as if that wasn't enough to sell a ticket to a movie lover, this movie is based on the outrageous true story of a black police officer, Detective Ron Stallworth, who infiltrated the Ku Klux Klan.

Are you kidding me?

Based on the trailers alone, I could tell this movie would be smart, funny, well-acted, and well-written, not to mention quite possibly the craziest true story I'd seen in a movie theater in a long time.

What I got was all that and more.

Right off the bat, this movie was a kick in the gut, specifically for any white, Christian person sitting in the reclining seats eating popcorn.

Jesus of Nazareth, the same man who I claim to follow, is also "followed" by people in the Ku Klux Klan?

They claim that Christ is the motivation behind their actions?

That in and of itself is enough for any person, let alone serious Christian, to be concerned.

But I kept watching.

The truth is I couldn't take my eyes off the screen.

This was more than a movie; this was a commentary on society today.

Not the 1800's, not the 1960's, but *today*.

This organization still exists.

And not only that, but perhaps even more dangerous is the fact that the Klan's way of thinking has seeped into the hearts and minds of people who aren't even aware of it.

This movie shows the ways in which racism and hatred have infiltrated our society, our systems of government, our schools, and our religions.

It pulls the curtain back to reveal what many people thought was just a part of our sad, ignorant past, is in fact as present as it ever has been.

The scary part is that it's hidden.

It's kept secret and it doesn't want to be revealed because we don't want it revealed.

Which brings me to the Black Lives Matter movement.

This is just one example of how the issues this movie and our faith are deeply intertwined.

A common reaction I hear to the Black Lives Matter movement is, "Well, I believe all lives matter."

You do?

Lets put that to the test.

If you were to turn on the TV to listen to any of the rich, famous, mega church pastors today, you would hear the following phrase uttered before too long…

"Just remember, God is for you!"

God is *for* you.

That sounds great, but it's also a little confusing.

When I'm watching baseball, I'm *for* the Boston Red Sox.

That means I'm *not* for the New York Yankees.

Which begs the question, if you're *for* one thing, can you be for another?

And if you're *for* this, are you *against* that?

Paul asks the Romans a fair question when he asks, "If God is for us, who is against us?"

Well a lot of things could be against us.

Does that mean God is against them?

What if they're praying to God too?

Does that mean God is *against* us?

I thought God was for us?

And if *all* lives matter then doesn't that include black lives?

Let's stop this ignorant response.

Sure, there are things and people that come against me all the time in life.

But I left this movie thinking to myself, "Nothing like *that* has ever come against me."

I've never had anyone try to harm my family because of the color of our skin.

I've never been systemically oppressed because of the way I look.

I've never known the fear of wearing certain things or going certain places because bad things happen to people like me.

So yeah, I do believe that all lives matter.

But I don't believe it needs to be said that all lives matter. Because society tends to know that some lives matter, while needing to be reminded that other lives matter, too.

This movie, along with the events of Charlottesville, Virginia in 2017, serve as a harsh reminder that sadly, some things still need to be said.

Things like, "Black lives matter."

And if you need a reminder, just watch this movie.

And if you need a reminder that God is for you, try being a reminder to others that God is for them.

Now, back to that intimate moment I was talking about.

As the credits rolled and I took a moment to collect myself after witnessing this powerful movie, I didn't ever think to actually take a look around.

So I did.

There was nobody in front of me, so I looked behind me.

One other person sat a few rows back on the opposite side of the theater.

I wasn't surprised.

The movie had been out for a few weeks and it was an early afternoon showtime in the middle of a weekday.

So, I grabbed my phone and my empty popcorn bucket, and made my way to the door.

As we exited the theater and entered into the lit hallway, I noticed the only other person leaving the theater.

He was an elderly black man with a walker and an empty bucket of popcorn, just like mine.

As we walked in silence down the long hallway, I wondered what he thought of the movie. How did it make him feel? He certainly must have had a different experience than I did.

I didn't say anything.

But as we walked out the front doors to make our way to our vehicles, we made eye contact, and at the same time, shook our heads and let out an audible sigh.

"Whew," I said.

He replied, "Yeah."

That was it.

It was like we both felt the weight of the past, present, and future all during the couple of hours we spent together in that theater.

It wasn't necessarily fun, although there were fun moments.

It wasn't necessarily sad, although there were sad moments.

It wasn't necessarily full of hope, although there were hopeful moments.

But that's church for you.

It is what it is.

And it's our job to respond accordingly.

Part III: Building a Community

Little Miss Sunshine (2006)

"Everyone, just... pretend to be normal."

- Richard Hoover

Love is patient; love is kind; love is not envious or boastful or arrogant or rude. It does not insist on its own way; it is not irritable or resentful; it does not rejoice in wrongdoing, but rejoices in the truth. It bears all things, believes all things, hopes all things, endures all things.

Love never ends. But as for prophecies, they will come to an end; as for tongues, they will cease; as for knowledge, it will come to an end. For we know only in part, and we prophesy only in part; but when the complete comes, the partial will come to an end. When I was a child, I spoke like a child, I thought like a child, I reasoned like a child; when I became an adult, I put an end to childish ways. For now we see in a mirror, dimly, but then we will see face to face. Now I know only in part; then I will know fully, even as I have been fully known. And now faith, hope, and love abide, these three; and the greatest of these is love.

- 1 Corinthians 13:4-13

For many of us, community is something into which we're born.

I was born into a fairly average-sized family that included a mom, dad, and eventually, a sister.

I had two sets of grandparents, a handful of aunts and uncles on both sides, and plenty of cousins to make the occasional family gathering seem like a pretty big event.

Family dynamics are some of the most common themes found in movies, but perhaps none are more accurate or hilariously relatable than the relationships in 2006's award-winning, *Little Miss Sunshine*.

This is the story of a family that includes the workaholic, motivated father, the hyper and overenthusiastic daughter, the teenage son going through life changes, the heartbroken, suicidal uncle with mental health issues, the inappropriate, outspoken, war veteran grandpa, and finally, the character my former professor would call the "Christ figure", the mother who cares for everyone and keeps the family together.

Whether or not those characters and their distinct personality traits seem familiar to you, they all represent the vastly different qualities and makeups that come with family structure.

Family is the community that many of us are lucky (or unlucky) enough to be born into. And whether you have a positive or negative experience, or somewhere in between, you'd most likely agree that family is a community unlike any other.

And some would actually consider "real" family to be the people we *do* choose to include in our lives.

Either way, family is the close-knit community of people about whom we deeply care and love. They're also the ones with whom life becomes complicated to navigate.

We all have family members with whom we don't mesh well.

We may even have family members we dislike.

We have family members who are our favorites and family member we simply tolerate.

We have family members who change. Sometimes people get older and aren't the "same person" they used to be. Sometimes they move away, get married, have kids, and the relationships are different.

Sometimes family members make choices with which we strongly disagree.

Uncle Frank, played by Steve Carell in a performance that is sweet, funny, and heartbreaking all at the same time, is the "black sheep" of this particular family.

We meet Frank in the beginning of the movie as he is recovering from a recent suicide attempt. He had fallen in love with one of his grad students who also happened to be male.

Now, at the time this movie was released, there hadn't been as much progress made concerning the acceptance of homosexual relationships as there has lately, but unfortunately, this situation is still relatable for many families today.

His sister, Sheryl, who is mostly shaken by his suicide attempt rather than his homosexuality, greets him warmly and welcomes him into her home. Then however, he is ridiculed by his brother-in-law, Richard, questioned by his curious niece, Olive, and made fun of by Richard's elderly father, Edwin.

These events lead the audience to believe this will be the central plot of the movie, however the real story begins when the characters lives start to become intertwined.

Olive decides she wants to try out for the "Little Miss Sunshine Pageant" but some of her family members don't consider her to be the "pageant type" because of her build and style. Richard is an aspiring author and motivational speaker, and Dwayne, Olive's brother, is striving to become a pilot.

As the family's goals and aspirations cause tension and drama during the road trip to the pageant in California, we see a very relatable and familiar drama unfold.

How do families support each other?

How do clashing personalities coexist?

What happens when a family experiences a tragedy?

How to they overcome obstacles together?

As this all plays out, we begin to see a clearer picture of the kind of love Christ calls us to have for our neighbors.

We see that while it may be difficult to love those who annoy us, who disagree with us, and who despise us, love is actually the healthier and more productive choice.

The family's differences begin to blur as they start focusing on what makes them family in the first place.

Their love for one another starts to bridge the gap between the disagreements, the hateful comments, and the judgmental mindsets.

No matter whom the people in this family have decided to be, they realize that this is the closest community they have, and they are going to love each other regardless of what makes them different.

Likewise, as followers of Christ, we are called to choose love within our own families, friend groups, work or school communities, and congregations, because these are the people we are doing life with closely.

These are the people who, no matter how different from us they are, it doesn't matter. Family is the community we cannot afford to fail.

Because the next step is even harder...

How do we love those we *don't have* to be around?

How do we love our distant neighbor?

Our community is just getting started.

Pitch Perfect (2012)

"You guys are the best. Even though some of you are pretty thin, I think you all have fat hearts. And that's what matters."

- Amy

Live in harmony with one another; do not be haughty, but associate with the lowly; do not claim to be wiser than you are. Do not repay anyone evil for evil, but take thought for what is noble in the sight of all. If it is possible, so far as it depends on you, live peaceably with all. Beloved, never avenge yourselves, but leave room for the wrath of God; for it is written, "Vengeance is mine, I will repay, says the Lord." No, "if your enemies are hungry, feed them; if they are thirsty, give them something to drink; for by doing this you will heap burning coals on their heads." Do not be overcome by evil, but overcome evil with good.

- Romans 12:16-21

In what is definitely the most irreverent movie I chose to include in this book, we are going to look at what might be the most difficult task when it comes to loving others and being part of a community.

Because while loving our enemies is hard, loving people we don't have to be around, or even think about, can be even harder.

What reason do we have to love the person at work with whom we never come into contact?

What reason do we possibly have to love the person at school we never pass in the hallway?

Why on earth does it matter if we love people around the world who aren't like us? Whether it's the people who disagree with us, people in different religions, or people from other countries, why does it matter if we love them?

They're not a part of our lives, let alone part of our communities.

Cant we just pretend they're not even there?

Well, sure.

But that's not what followers of Jesus would do.

This is the part of being a Christian that is a pain in the neck.

It seems pointless, hard, and a waste of time.

But that's exactly why is was a priority for Jesus and should be a priority for anyone who claims to follow his way of life.

Jesus sought those who were hungry, thirsty, naked, and homeless, so that he could lend a helping hand.

Jesus wanted people who were outcasts to be included.

Jesus cared for those who nobody else would.

And as a church, that is hard to do when we just flat-out, dislike certain "types" of people.

I know Christians who just don't like "liberals" or "crazy right-wing" people.

I know Christians who don't like gay people.

I know Christians who don't like Muslims.

And we already covered the fact that there are sadly, still Christians who don't like people because of the color of their skin.

In fact, you name a "type" of person and I could probably name a "Christian" who doesn't care much for that person.

How can we fix this?

Well, first we should start by acknowledging that this is not a new problem.

Then, we can look to someone who already tried to deal with it.

In his letter to the Romans, Paul told them to "live in harmony with one another."

What does that mean?

I'll give you a hint.

It doesn't mean to just tolerate someone.

And it doesn't mean its okay to hate certain kinds of people, either.

This is where the "Barden Bellas" can help us out.

Pitch Perfect is a movie about a group of girls who attend the fictional, Barden University.

The Bellas, an a cappella singing group, spend most of the movie practicing and competing in a cappella singing competitions against other groups, both from their own school and surrounding schools, as well as participating in typical collegiate activities and functions.

The young women in the group are a comical representation of the many different kinds of people one might encounter at a university. The group includes typical stereotypes as well as seemingly random quirks and traits assigned to create the most outlandish group of girls imaginable.

As the girls get to know each other and go through some of the more common struggles that any new group of friends might encounter, their singing is mostly remarkable.

They sing a cappella renditions of some classics as well as modern pop and hip-hop songs.

And the one thing that stands out as being nearly "pitch-perfect" in their singing, is also the one thing that needs work when it comes to their relationships within the group.

Harmony.

These ladies can harmonize with the best.

But when their personalities and differences start to clash, they are anything but in sync.

You know how when people in a church group, a work group, or any kind of group try to get everyone on the same page, but instead they sort of clash instead?

I imagine a church boardroom during a heated conversation.

Or a political debate during the primaries when there are like 10 people on stage, all of them arguing with each other, when in the end, they all pretty much want the same thing.

On a much larger scale, I imagine society trying to force everyone to be a certain way, when all it does is make people frustrated and angry that they can't simply control one another.

Why can't everyone just be the same, and look the same, and think the same, and believe all the same things?

We would all be on the same page and we'd all be singing the same note!

Wouldn't that sound great?

Yeah, I guess it could, but have you ever heard a song when people are singing in harmony?

Have you ever heard the National Anthem performed by a quartet, rather than someone just singing a solo?

There's something beautiful about harmony.

Four different notes sung at the same time, none of them the same, but all of them blending together beautifully...

Here's an example.

Get online and search for Jimmy Fallon and Billy Joel singing harmony.

Billy Joel has one of the best voices of all time.

That's not just my opinion; it's a fact.

And during one of his appearances on *The Tonight Show Starring Jimmy Fallon,* Billy and Jimmy perform a famous song using an app that loops their voices over and over.

One by one, they each start singing a line of the song, and looping it so that it continues to play while the other one sings the next line.

The end result is much better than I expected the first time I watched it.

They're both singing completely different parts of the harmony, and when they take their individual turns, it sounds fine, but when they loop their voices together, it's incredible.

It's like Paul was writing to the Romans.

He didn't say live together in "melody" with one another.

He didn't say that everyone needed to get on the same page because that's the only way the church could work.

No, instead, he recognized that there would be minor and major differences.

People would look different, act different, think different, believe different, and come from all different places, and yet they were trying to be one church.

One community.

It might have seemed impossible at times, just like it still does to us.

But Jesus gave us the example, and Paul gave us the reminder, that we're not expected to be the same.

So we need to get that idea out of our heads and start focusing on the actual goal.

We need to do better at living in harmony.

We need to do better at acknowledging each other's differences and complimenting them in way that give them a purpose in the community.

We need to love others in a way that proclaims, not only that they are indeed welcome, but also there is a place specifically for them.

Jesus sat at a table with tax collectors, sinners, and people who would betray him.

There is a place at that table for everyone.

<u>Avengers: Infinity War (2018)</u>

"That's too high a price."
- Scarlet Witch

"Only you have the power to pay it."
- Vision

For just as the body is one and has many members, and all the members of the body, though many, are one body, so it is with Christ. For in the one Spirit we were all baptized into one body—Jews or Greeks, slaves or free—and we were all made to drink of one Spirit.

Indeed, the body does not consist of one member but of many. If the foot would say, "Because I am not a hand, I do not belong to the body," that would not make it any less a part of the body. And if the ear would say, "Because I am not an eye, I do not belong to the body," that would not make it any less a part of the body. If the whole body were an eye, where would the hearing be? If the whole body were hearing, where would the sense of smell be? But as it is, God arranged the members in the body, each one of them, as he chose. If all were a single member, where would the body be? As it is, there are many members, yet one body. The eye cannot say to the hand, "I have no need of you," nor again the head to the feet, "I have no need of you." On the contrary, the members of the body that seem to be weaker are indispensable, and those members of the body that we think less honorable we clothe with greater honor, and our less respectable members are treated with greater respect; whereas our more respectable members do not need this. But God has so arranged the body, giving the greater honor to the inferior member, that there may be no dissension within the body, but the members may have the same care for one another. If one member suffers, all suffer together with it; if one member is honored, all rejoice together with it.

- 1 Corinthians 12:12-26

I know this technically belongs in the "Blockbuster" section, however, I saw a story about the church so clearly in this movie that I couldn't ignore it.

But first, let's just reflect on what a blast this movie was right up until the last couple minutes, shall we?

I love comic book movies as much as everyone else these days, and this is one of my favorites, but I will be the first to admit when a movie is not what I expected.

Typically, most "superhero" movies stick to somewhat of a simple formula.

The hero fights the villain and wins in the end.

I think its fair to say this movie did *not* stick to the formula.

From start to finish, the story was all over the place (in a good way).

It was so fun watching all these characters which most of us have spent the better part of a decade getting to know in other movies, pop up onscreen with another character with whom they had never interacted before.

Again, it was a blast to watch unfold.

Until it wasn't...

You know what I'm talking about.

It was an awkward silence to say the least as everyone in the theater experienced something we hadn't before in the Marvel Cinematic Universe. We watched as half of our favorite characters disappeared from existence. And we felt the loss.

So, as I sat on a flight from Cincinnati back home to Oklahoma City a few months after *Infinity War* was released, I re-watched it for the first time since seeing it in theaters.

I pressed play with hesitation because I've always had a hard time giving "sad movies" a second viewing.

But I didn't hesitate long because this isn't a sad movie.

This is a fun movie and it's one that is just as much about hope as it is loss.

Ultimately this is a movie about fighting the good fight.

But we've seen that before.

This time was different.

This time it was deeply personal.

In the history of filmmaking, (as far as I know) there has never been *10 years* of movies, all building storylines, developing characters, and leading to a singular climax, in what could only be described as a cinematic event... let alone with the promise of more to come.

So, as I watched with anticipation, expecting to be taken for a ride and to "escape" for the next few hours, I couldn't help but notice it right away.

I wouldn't be able to escape this time.

I was in church again.

And in the most action-packed, blockbuster, summer popcorn movie of the year, I began to see the church reflected onscreen.

As the story jumped from one location to the next, focusing on one group of characters after another, and giving all our favorite heroes a different objective or purpose, I began to understand the big picture of what Christ's church looks like.

On one planet, we watched as two strong, yet snarky leaders in Iron Man and Doctor Strange argued with one another about what to do next, all while the overly-anxious teenager, Spider-Man struggled to find his place in the battle. In the midst of chaos, all he wanted was to do the right thing, to know his purpose, and to have the respect and affirmation of his elders. But they made it clear who was and who wasn't in charge.

That's what the church looks like sometimes.

Meanwhile, on a ship in outer space, we watched the Guardians of the Galaxy, a small band of misfits who care for each other, but had been together so long they bickered like siblings, meet a newcomer in Thor, who was not like them. Could he be trusted?

Could he fit in? What could he have to offer? Could they benefit from him? All these were questions they asked each other before welcoming their new passenger, when all he wanted was a companion on his journey, and possibly a friend as he grieved a tremendous loss.

Sadly, that's what the church looks like sometimes.

Finally, back on Earth, the remaining heroes were spending most of their time together calculating the next move. In meeting, after meeting, after meeting, Captain America, Scarlet Witch, Vision, and Black Panther all took part in a larger debate about the strategy to be used in the upcoming fight. And after what seemed like *far* too much time spent talking about it, the Avengers finally took action in a valiant effort, only to come up short in the end.

Unfortunately, that's what the church looks like sometimes.

If you had invested as much in these characters over the years as I had, you felt several feelings as this movie came to an end.

It was fun, but you felt incomplete.

You felt loss.

You were left wanting more.

You needed answers.

You were impatient, immediately thinking about how long you had to wait until the next one.

It was going to be a *long* year.

Regarding the church, what do you think the disciples and all the followers of Jesus felt after Jesus was crucified?

Even after he was resurrected and ascended to heaven, it seemed like the "church" was left with more questions than answers.

Sure, Jesus changed the world and all of their lives for the better, but there's a glaring question on everyone's minds.

What's next?

I mean the church *has* to go on, right?

Everyone has to move forward eventually.

What does the future hold?

And while we've come a long way since the days of the early church, how far have we come?

I've only been in full-time ministry for ten years, but I already know one thing for sure. Christians will always have issues. The church will always have issues. And more often than not, we're left sitting around tables at board meetings wondering what is the next move.

And where is God in all this?

When churches have drama, is God in the midst of that?

When pastors are betrayed or churches are forced to make difficult decisions, was God on some distant planet dealing with something else?

And perhaps the scariest question on all our minds is, "What happens to the church now?"

Some churches close their doors.

What questions did they ask?

How are they left to pick up the pieces and think about the future?

Why didn't God *do something?*

I'm going to turn to an unexpected place.

A parable found in the non-canonical Gospel of Thomas.

Now, before you ask yourself, how can these words be trusted? If it's not in the Bible, is it the real word of God?

Those are valid questions.

First, I would ask if God is limited to speaking only through scriptures in the Biblical canon.

I don't think so.

Second, just hear the words of the story.

I think there's something to be gained regardless.

The parable, just like the canonical parables of Jesus, tells of the kingdom of heaven, which is compared to a woman carrying a jar full of meal.

While the woman was walking down a road, far from home, the handle of the jar broke and the meal emptied out behind her on the road. She eventually reaches her house, not having realized that anything had spilled, and she set the jar down only to find it empty.

The account of this story can be found in *Thomas 97.*
Now, you're probably asking the same question I was after reading it for the first time.

"And?"

So, she got home and the jar was empty? Then what? What happens next?

The answer is simple.

Nothing happens next.

For the woman and for the reader, nothing happens next.

Now, if this were to happen in reality, *something* would happen next.

Even if the woman just went about her day, at least that is something.

But as far as the story goes, that's the end.

So, what's the takeaway?

Nothing.

Sometimes God is present in nothing.

Sometimes God is present in loss.

Sometimes God doesn't require a silver lining because loss is loss and it is supposed to hurt.

Sometimes we come up short, both as Christians and as human beings.

Sometimes churches don't accomplish their mission.

Sometimes Christians sin.

Sometimes followers of Jesus don't act much like they're following anyone, let alone Christ.

And sometimes we can put a lot of thought, and planning, and meetings, and money, and even prayer behind a mission.

Sometimes it *still* doesn't turn out like we'd hoped.

Does that mean God wasn't present?

No, it doesn't.

God has been present throughout the course of history when all kinds of things have gone wrong.

We were all created in the image of God and we all have something only we can offer the world when it needs to be reminded of God's presence.

The church is the result of a number of different people doing a number of different things in order to show the love of God to the world.

It looks like the Avengers when there are heroes on one planet doing one thing, while people on another planet are doing another thing, and at the same time others are in another place doing other things.

And as hard as it is to accept, sometimes it's not about the end result, as much as it is about offering the world God's love the best way you know how, and in the specific way you were created.

It's a high price to pay.

Only you have the power to pay it.

Coco (2017)

"If there's no one left in the living world to remember you, you disappear from this world. But you can change that!"

- Héctor

For I received from the Lord what I also handed on to you, that the Lord Jesus on the night when he was betrayed took a loaf of bread, and when he had given thanks, he broke it and said, "This is my body that is for you. Do this in remembrance of me." In the same way he took the cup also, after supper, saying, "This cup is the new covenant in my blood. Do this, as often as you drink it, in remembrance of me."

- 1 Corinthians 11:23-25

Well, here we are.

This is our last step in Christian community building, and it begins with asking a difficult question.

How do we approach end-of-life issues as a family? Or a group of friends? Or a church congregation? And doesn't that sort of come with the territory?

One would think that Christian communities would be experts in approaching the topic of death.

But for some, death is their greatest fear.

For others, thoughts of heaven and hell encapsulate what they believe about the afterlife.

And for many, death is one of those topics we simply brush to the side.

"I'll think about it when it gets closer to time," we tell ourselves.

But regardless of what we think we know or what we choose to believe about death, the end of a person's life is an inevitable part of life in a Christian community, or any community for that matter.

That's the cold, hard truth.

It's sad, depressing, and just plain hard to think about.

So, who better than the fine people at Walt Disney Pictures and Pixar Animation Studios to help us deal with our emotionally complicated issues? (They're actually really good at that.)

Coco is an animated movie that my daughter laughs at and sings along with, while I enjoy watching until the last 20 minutes, at which point I find a chore that needs done or even just an excuse to leave the room. Anything is better than crying over children's cartoon.

But this story is much more than a kid's movie.

It's a sweet, funny, deeply spiritual movie about family and how we choose to remember our loved ones who have passed away.

Specifically, it focuses on a family in Mexico during the Día de los Muertos, or Day of the Dead, celebration.

In the movie, 12-year-old Miguel is an aspiring musician in a family who forbids him to have anything to do with it. Miguel's great-great-grandmother Imelda was left alone with her 3-year-old daughter Coco (Miguel's great grandmother) after her husband supposedly left to pursue a music career.

Miguel, unwilling to let go of his dream, tries to enter a talent show on the Day of the Dead, but he first decides to steal the guitar of the late, famous musician, Ernesto de la Cruz's mausoleum, because his grandmother destroyed his guitar.

As a result of stealing from the dead, Miguel becomes cursed to the Land of the Dead. He must then receive a blessing from a deceased family member's ghost before he can return to the Land of the Living.

On Day of the Dead, deceased people can visit the Land of the Living (although they're invisible to people still alive) as long as their family or loved ones "remember" them by placing their photo on a table called an *ofrenda.*

We find that Miguel's great-great-grandfather did not, in fact, run away, but rather Ernesto de la Cruz murdered him, so that Ernesto could steal his songs and become a famous musician.

Miguel must clear his grandfather's name, not only so his family will once again place his photo on the *ofrenda*, but also so that he'll be remembered with honor and be reunited with his daughter Coco.

That might all be confusing if you haven't seen this movie, but trust me, there's not a dry eye in the house during the last 20 minutes or so.

This movie evokes a powerful emotional response to the idea that while some of us will be remembered, we might not necessarily be remembered for what we'd like. And while some of us won't necessarily be forgotten, it is up to our surviving loved ones to carry on our memory.

Now, the idea of a legacy might not be important to everyone.

But to witness a story of a man who was wrongfully accused of abandoning his family, when in reality, all he wanted was to care for them, it certainly can wake us up to what is really important in life, as well as the fact that we only have one chance to do the right thing.

It also shines a light on an important part of community building, one that even if we don't always realize it, makes our communities complete…

Our loved ones who have passed on.

What roles do the departed play in our communities?

Some people are remembered well, while some are certainly not.

Some people's presence is felt even more after they're gone, which begs the question, are they really ever gone?

Coco again shines a light on the truth that as long as people are remembered, not just in our hearts and minds, but also in our words, our actions, and our conversations, they are in fact still a valuable part of our communities.

The Christian Church, along with many other denominations, participates in All Saints' Day, which is a holiday commemorating the bond between those in Heaven and those still on Earth.

But where and when are your loved ones, those who have passed away, still the most present?

Maybe it's the memory of a grandparent's house on Christmas.

Maybe it's in old family photos scattered throughout the house.

Maybe it's in a certain song that brings back specific memories, or even a smell that reminds you of being in the presence of someone you love.

Whatever it is, may we continue to remember those we've lost, but also may we be intentional about keeping their memory alive.

The characters in this movie make it a point to celebrate memories as part of their community. They talk about their relatives, they honor them with gestures, and they make their presence known.

Jesus, on the night he was handed over, met with his friends for a meal.

He took a loaf of bread, and after he blessed it, he broke it and said that it was his body given for them.

For as often as they were to eat of this bread, he asked that they remember him.

After supper he took a cup, he poured the wine, and made with them a new covenant. This cup was a symbol of what had been poured out for many for the forgiveness of sin.

And as often as they would drink of that cup, they were to do so in remembrance of him.

Just like it is when we meet together for meals, when we welcome others to the table of Christ, we sometimes wonder *who* is indeed welcome.

Who are our neighbors?

They're our family, our friends, and our church congregation.

They're our acquaintances, our co-workers, and all the people we don't even know.

They're our enemies, people from foreign countries, and people with whom we disagree.

They're our loved ones who have passed away and those who are forever in our hearts.

And finally, Jesus, who also sits at the table, welcomes us.

There is a place for you and a place for me.

May we never forget it.

Bonus Content: TV Shows

The Office (2005-2013)

"I think an ordinary paper company like Dunder-Mifflin was a great subject for a documentary. There's a lot of beauty in ordinary things. Isn't that kind of the point?"

- Pam

Now faith is the assurance of things hoped for, the conviction of things not seen. Indeed, by faith our ancestors received approval. By faith we understand that the worlds were prepared by the word of God, so that what is seen was made from things that are not visible.

- Hebrews 11:1-3

I didn't have Netflix growing up.

If we wanted to watch a TV show from start to finish, we had to either purchase the show on DVD or watch it every week on live television.

So, there was something I had never done before.

I had never watched a TV show in its entirety. That is until my senior year of high school when I stumbled upon a show so awkward and dry and genius that I couldn't turn away.

My friend and I had watched the movie *Anchorman* in the theater and I thought Steve Carell was the funniest human alive. So, while we were browsing around a local entertainment store, I saw him on the cover of what appeared to be a TV show and bought it immediately.

We went home and had what would become my first binge-watching experience ever. We barreled through the first season of *The Office* and were instantly hooked.

Now, at the time I was not aware of the influence this show would have on my entire life up to this very moment, but it would soon become clear. I laughed harder at this show, and was more invested in it, than anything I'd ever seen up to that point.

Michael Scott, the bumbling office manager with no filter, might be the least self-aware character in television history.

Jim was the handsome, lovable, carefree salesman, who simply had nothing better to do than work at Dunder Mifflin, prank his co-worker, and flirt with the receptionist.

Dwight was the recipient of those pranks, but was also the loyal-to-a-fault "Assistant *to the* Regional Manager" and would annoy anybody in any workplace.

Pam was the quiet, reserved, artistic receptionist who felt like the glue that literally kept the office from falling apart by hiding Michael's screw-ups, keeping Jim from going insane, and being the voice of reason for the audience every week.

The characters, like the show, were hard not to love.

And for nine years of my life, I was along for the ride.

When I was in college, moving from city to city, whether I was having a great week or was incredibly stressed out, I usually tuned in on Thursday nights. Or I recorded it.

I remember watching this show with friends from different places, some of with whom I no longer keep in contact.

My first day at the University of Oklahoma, I made a friend because we both responded to someone by saying, "That's what she said."

A lifelong bond was formed.

I remember one year, there was an ice storm that took out most of the power in Norman, Oklahoma, and kept students stranded in their dorms or apartments for a few days. But my friend's apartment had a generator, so we were able to catch that week's episode. We laughed until we cried, and that remains my favorite episode of the series: *Dinner Party.* If you've seen it, you know what I'm talking about.

I remember watching the show as it was winding down in its final seasons. I had graduated college and was working my first full-time job. *The Office* still had a way of making me laugh and helping me unwind after a long week.

Even after I got married, my wife (who is not a fan of that particular brand of humor) tolerated my Thursday night tradition right up until the finale.

Another friend of mine, also a minister, came over for a watch-party. We laughed hard and we both had minor allergies as the credits rolled for the last time. Or maybe they were tears, I honestly can't remember...

A near-decade was spent with the employees of Dunder Mifflin Paper Company from Scranton, Pennsylvania. And then it was over.

Or was it?

Ten years after the premiere of *The Office,* I found myself working at a church in Duncan, Oklahoma. Part of my job was to teach the high school Sunday School class every Sunday morning.

Sunday School in 2014 was a hard sell.

No high school students want to wake up for a Bible study, let alone *before* church, but it was my job to teach them if they did.

So, I decided to get creative.

A small group of students and I started a new form of studying Christianity on Sunday mornings.

What better way to study how to practice the Christian faith in normal, mundane, everyday life, than to watch an episode of *The Office*?

We would watch an episode, talk about the characters and their actions, and think about the way people interact in a modern workplace, or school in their case.

Then we would think about a question.

What would Jesus do?

I know, you've probably heard that before and ignored it.

But, seriously...

How would Jesus respond to this random situation from this sitcom that has no relation or connection to the Bible or really any Holy Scripture?

You might think this could work with any TV show, or movie, or book, etc. And it probably could. But not as good as it works with this one.

The Office takes a look at the ordinary, daily lives of a group of co-workers, some who are friends, and some who are not. It's boring and it's regular. But there's something special about it…

It's almost as if there's a magnifying glass on their world.

Everyone is a character you have probably encountered in your daily routine, except on the show those personalities are magnified.

Some people might say, "My boss is bad, but he's not *that* bad."

"That guy at my school is annoying, but he's not *that annoying.*"

"That girl I work with is tightly-wound, but not *that* tightly-wound."

Or even, "I want to tell you about this guy at work but I just can't explain him. Oh wait, he's kind of like Andy Bernard from *The Office.*"

Now here's a sentence you've probably never read before.

The Office, in a way, did what Jesus did.

Jesus would tell stories and parables about situations which people could understand. They could relate to what he was saying, so much at times that they probably thought they could predict what he was going to say next.

But then Jesus would flip the script. There would come a twist somewhere in the story. It would become an extreme example of the way Jesus taught how the world should work.

It became easier to understand, but difficult to learn.

If you want to see perhaps the best example of modern day misconceptions and ignorance about racism, go watch the episode of *The Office* titled "Diversity Day" and make sure to take notes.

Now, even with all that being said, you would probably get some resistance if you tried to use this show for a Sunday School curriculum.

"It has bad words!"

"It makes sexual references."

"It's way too inappropriate for church."

I disagree.

What is inappropriate is that the church of Jesus Christ can sometimes have more of a problem with curse words than contributing to the much larger issues in the world.

The Office made an impact because it shocked people.

The characters, mainly the boss, would say and do things that caught our attention. And we laughed because we know someone like that, or maybe because we were suddenly aware of ourselves.

If Christians continue to live in a bubble and make it our mission to get the rest of the world to join us in that bubble, then Jesus' message will continue to go unheard.

If we continue to be less and less shocked by Jesus' teachings, and continue warming up to the feel-good stuff instead, then we're in danger of losing sight of the Kingdom of Heaven.

So, the next time you're watching your favorite show on a certain night of the week, do yourself a favor.

Don't just zone out and get lost in the entertainment.

Think.

Let yourself be taught by something you didn't think had anything to offer.

You might be surprised.

To quote the great Michael Scott,

"Fool me once, strike one. But fool me twice... strike three."

LOST (2004 – 2010)

"I don't believe in destiny."
-   Jack Shephard

"Yes, you do. You just don't know it yet."
-   John Locke

Here's an example of a show that completely messed with my mind every time I watched an episode.

I'm talking about ABC's award-winning mystery/drama show *LOST.*

Talk about a philosophical piece of television.

This was a show that dealt mostly with a diverse cast of characters and the growth they experienced together following a plane crash on a mysterious, deserted island.

But as the show went on, every season challenged viewers to ask more profound questions than the last. The show, which seemed to dive deeper every year into life's hard topics, disguised itself as a mystery about a group of strangers.

When it fact, the mystery was the collection of life's most complex and philosophical, unanswered questions, most of which were *left* unanswered.

And the predominant idea that lingered over all six seasons (right up until the final episode) was this...

Everything happens for a reason.

If you've been on social media within the last 30 seconds or so, you've probably seen that quote.

Trust me,

Someone has posted it.

If you've experienced some kind of heartbreak due to a loss in your life, whether it was the death of a loved one, or the end of a relationship, then chances are you have heard someone say, "It's all part of God's plan."

If you have ever been discouraged about anything at all, I'd be willing to bet that you have come across this familiar phrase in one form or another.

I have.

I hate it.

This idea was instilled in me from a young age. Anytime someone tries to make anyone feel better, this is usually his or her advice. And even if it's coming from a place of love, it needs to stop.

Anytime there is a disaster, like the bombing of the Murrah Building in Oklahoma City, the terrorist attacks on September 11, 2001, or Hurricane Katrina, the idea of God's "plan" immediately gets thrown into the discussion. Yet for some reason, I've never felt even a little bit better after hearing it.

Ever.

So, why is that?

Does God know the future?

I think so, because God is surely not limited by time.

Does God have a plan for the future?

I think so, because Jesus clearly had ideas for the way the world should work.

Did God's plan require everything in the world to happen exactly like it has, even if that thing was horrible?

I don't know about that.

It is hard for me to envision God devising a plan that involves the tragic deaths of thousands of people.

And yet, people like to use that logic at times.

"It's all part of God's plan."

Really?

So, let's get this straight.

For the Creator of the universe to carry out this plan, someone had to fly a plane into a building filled with people?

Someone just *had* to walk into a school with a gun for the plan to work out?

Someone must continually commit horrible act after horrible act for God's plan to come to fruition?

That doesn't seem like a great plan.

But I do believe God is a good God.

So, why do bad things happen?

They happen because our plans are not always synchronized with God's plans. We have free will to do whatever we want, even if it's not part of the plan. In fact, I don't think God is very happy with the way certain things go down sometimes.

So, that is how I came to believe that everything *doesn't* happen for a reason.

Don't get me wrong, there used to be a time when I did.

I used to think it sounded like a nice idea.

I mean, who wouldn't want to believe in destiny? Who wouldn't want to believe that everything happens for a specific reason? It would be fantastic if every bad thing that happened had a purpose behind it, and if that purpose eventually made every situation seem better. That's what we all want to believe. But somewhere along the way I stopped being able to swallow that pill.

That is, until lately.

There was a spark of hope in me recently that I haven't felt for a long time. The concept of destiny has always made me confused and annoyed because of how I understood it. But recently I saw destiny played out in the life of another person in a way that made sense to me.

For the first time, it happened in a way that connects with the God I believe in.

Could it be possible that God has a plan that is less specific in the details than we'd like it to be?

Could God be drawing us to something, some purpose, that isn't entirely decided yet?

I realized that maybe God *does* have a plan, but we are fully capable of screwing it all up or carrying it out.

Could God just be waiting on us for the plan to come together?

I'm a big believer in free will. Anyone reading this can choose his or her very next move at any moment. Does God plan that move? I don't think so.

But is God drawing us to make a certain move in our lives eventually? I can buy that.

Actually, I know that to be true. That thing God uses to draw us to make certain decisions is called compassion. It's caring about something or someone.

And *that* is God's will.

That is God's calling.

That's the plan that Jesus' actions revealed.

I used to work with kids, teenagers, and young adults on a daily basis. I saw a lot of decisions being made. Some were good, some were bad, and some were neither. But I love watching someone go through the decision-making process.

When Jesus made decisions, we got to see what it looked like to be "led" by the Spirit into making certain decisions. So, when I see people living in that same Holy Spirit of Christ, I see a change in them.

They start to produce *fruits* of the Spirit.

I see a change in what drives them and a change in what pulls on their hearts.

I see a change in what they care about and in their priorities. This is an example of what I saw happen in someone's life a few years ago.

See, there's a moment when a person realizes what hearing God's voice feels like. You can almost see the walls being torn down inside them when it happens and they become filled with peace. It's like they realize what God's plan is all about, even without knowing the future.

Because it's not about the future…

It's about the present.

Then, one by one, you notice that person's small, daily decisions start to change. Decisions like how to act, how to react, how to speak, how to listen, how to respond, how to see the world, and how to live.

But how can God use someone's crazy, difficult, and sometimes heartbreaking life to bring them to this point?

It happens when everything doesn't make sense, and that's okay.

It happens when we can't find a reason for everything, and that's okay too.

So, is it possible that some things do happen for a reason?

Or perhaps, for a purpose?

Yes.

Not because God mapped it all out for us, but because we have the choice and the ability to *give* things a reason.

When I saw this happen to someone other than myself, I was capable of looking at it from a different perspective than I had before.

I saw God, not as a puppet master controlling our every move, but more like someone playing a song that we are all a part of.

Sometimes it sounds good, sometimes it doesn't. But the music never stops, and we're the ones playing. It's our responsibility to find the right key, the right pitch, and the right harmony.

God is always directing us, guiding us, and helping us to see and hear the world through the eyes and ears of Christ.

Do we always have to be followers?

No.

But why wouldn't we want to, when God is leading us to something better.

A better life? Not necessarily.

But a better way? Absolutely.

Now, if someone tells me that everything happens for a reason, I usually just smile and nod my head in affirmation.

I guess it might.

What I am sure of is the fact that I am called to a certain purpose.

And even though sometimes I wish I could, I can't seem to avoid it.

Maybe it's destiny.

Comedians in Cars Getting Coffee (2012 – Present)

"That simple thing of like, 'Let's have a catch; spend your time with me for a second,' is so insanely ingrained in us… 'Just a moment with me.' Just give me a moment."

- Jim Carrey, _Comedians in Cars Getting Coffee_

Let us hold fast to the confession of our hope without wavering, for he who has promised is faithful. And let us consider how to provoke one another to love and good deeds, not neglecting to meet together, as is the habit of some, but encouraging one another, and all the more as you see the Day approaching.

- Hebrews 10: 23-25

What is the *best* part of life?

Someone once asked me that question, and I immediately started thinking of big, extravagant events.

"I don't know, maybe vacations?" I said, just trying to think of an acceptable response.

After all, there are a lot of things that I really love about life.

Christmas, water parks, going to the movies, traveling, binge-watching a TV show, trying new, adventurous foods, the list goes on and on…

But the more I thought about it, the more that list felt like just another generic response to the question. Because the best times I've had in the last few years haven't been doing those things.

Recently, I've become less and less interested in big events. Yes, attending the occasional football game or concert is a lot of fun. And I love spending a week on vacation with my family, or at a camp or mission trip with church groups in the summertime. But sometime along the way, I lost my excitement for big events, and I wasn't sure why.

The weird thing is that I love spending time with people more than ever, but I lost the passion and zeal I once possessed for extravagant outings. I realized that a lot of the times, people are what I get excited about anymore.

Just *being with* people has contributed to my enjoyment in life, as well as my faith, in one way or another.

And God showed up in another unexpected place to shine a light on this revelation, which has helped me to live more intentionally when it comes to how I spend my time.

This show is called *Comedians in Cars Getting Coffee* starring Jerry Seinfeld. On the surface, it sounds like it could be the most boring show of all time. Every episode is roughly 20 minutes long and starts with stand-up comedian Jerry Seinfeld finding an old classic vehicle, picking up another famous comedian or celebrity, and the two of them proceed to have a conversation at a local restaurant or coffee shop.

It sounds a little dull, right?

Well I binge-watched every episode in a span of about a week, and I couldn't figure out why it fascinated me so much. Then it clicked. I realized the connection between the show and the new way I had been living my life.

During one episode, Jerry is leaving the local coffee shop with his guest, fellow stand-up comedian Sarah Silverman, and as they're walking toward the car they decide to make a spontaneous stop at a nearby donut shop. You can tell that Jerry felt the need to justify an unplanned trip to get donuts as he laughs to himself and makes a declaration…

"I've figured out that the 'non-event' is the best part of life."

I had to pause the episode for a moment.

The non-event? What does that even mean?

Well, it's exactly what it sounds like. Non-events are the things we do in life that are not only unplanned, but they're not much of anything at all.

The non-event is the time spent with family in the vehicle on the *way* to an event.

The non-event is sitting on your front porch just to take a break from the day.

The non-event is spontaneously having a cup of coffee with a friend, just to talk about nothing.

Jerry's self-titled sitcom, *Seinfeld,* was always referred to as "a show about nothing." His new show is about the same thing, maybe even more so, but it is so captivating in its simplicity.

The beauty of the non-event is found in spending a moment with another person, and going for a cup of coffee is the perfect example.

It is nothing more than a sometimes unplanned, in the moment, unscheduled break from the day, with the bonus of friendly conversation. I rarely write in my weekly schedule, "coffee with so-and-so" because most of the time, someone calls or texts and says, "Hey, let's go get coffee!"

I never turn it down.

There are times working in a church when a person will stop by the office to chat, even if it's just for 15 minutes. And when I look back on a typical workday, those are the conversations I remember most. Those are the parts of the day that seem most meaningful.

As I'm getting older, I'm beginning to realize the value of the non-event, and it's not because I can all of a sudden relax or because I don't like doing activities, but actually quite the opposite.

I appreciate the non-event because those are the times you share with a person, or people, or even yourself.

The non-event takes the focus off the event and places it on the people you're with.

It can happen anywhere or anytime.

We get so caught up in trying to plan the most exciting vacations, or attending the coolest concerts, or going to the biggest games, and we sometimes forget the value of sharing a moment with someone.

Time is the most valuable thing we have, and unlike money, we can't save it for later.

We have no choice but to spend every minute of every day as we go through it. We can plan and schedule and try to predict what is going to happen every week for the rest of our lives, but when you get the rare opportunity to share a moment with another person, one that wasn't planned and is full of conversation about nothing, remember to pause and enjoy it.

I want to spend my time *and* money interacting with my favorite people. Spending $100 on some form of entertainment could be fun, but spending a few bucks on a cup of coffee and conversation with a friend could be priceless.

Seinfeld claimed that the non-event is the best part of life.

I think he's right.

Acknowledgements

First, a special 'thank you' to my family, especially my wife, Meghan, and my daughters, Keely and Kennedy, for putting up with watching more movies than you ever wanted to, but also for being a source of constant love and support. I love you.

I want to thank my Mom, Dad, Ali, Kale, Meme, and all my aunts, uncles, cousins, and in-laws for all of the love (and movie trips) over the years. Also, I need to give a shout-out to my most consistent movie partners (besides my wife), Matt Parcher, Robin Hobson, Monty Moery, and my dad every time a new *Star Wars* movie comes out.

Finally, I want to thank a few more special people without whom this book would not be possible. Thank you to my youth group from the Christian Church in Duncan for (unknowingly) being the inspiration behind this project in the beginning. Thanks to the person I've always considered my pastor, Rev. Sondra Ladd, for investing so much in me. Thanks to Pastors Chris Muse, Derrick Marshall, Rev. Michael Davison and Rev. Shannon Cook for your unwavering friendship and support in ministry. Thank you to Rev. Ronnie Fields for being my colleague in leading our "Faith and Film" workshop every summer. If I write another one of these, *Tommy Boy* will be included for sure. And thanks to the First Christian Church in Hennessey. I am lucky to be your pastor. Love you all!

Credits

Franklin, S. & Aronofsky, D. (2014). *Noah*. United States: Paramount Pictures.

Kurtz, G. & Lucas, G. (1977). *Star Wars: Episode IV – A New Hope*. United States: 20th Century Fox.

Kennedy, K. & Abrams, J. (2015). *Star Wars: The Force Awakens*. United States: Walt Disney Studios Motion Pictures.

Donner L. S. & Singer, B. (2014). *X-Men: Days of Future Past*. United States & United Kingdom: 20th Century Fox.

Thomas, E. & Nolan, C. (2008). *The Dark Knight*. United States & United Kingdom: Warner Bros. Pictures.

Keach, J. & Mangold, J. (2015). *Walk the Line*. United States: 20th Century Fox.

Owen, A. & Hancock, J. L. (2013). *Saving Mr. Banks*. Australia, United Kingdom, & United States: Walt Disney Studios Motion Pictures.

Marshall, F. & Eastwood, C. (2016). *Sully*. United States: Warner Bros. Pictures.

Blum, J. & Lee, S. (2018). *BlacKkKlansman*. United States: Focus Features.

Turtletaub, M., Dayton, J., & Faris, V. (2006). *Little Miss Sunshine*. United States: Fox Searchlight Pictures.

Brooks, P. & Moore, J. (2012). *Pitch Perfect*. United States: Universal Pictures

Feige, K., Russo, A., & Russo, J. (2018). *Avengers: Infinity War*. United States: Walt Disney Studios Motion Pictures.

Anderson, D. & Unkrich, L. (2017). *Coco*. United States: Walt Disney Studios Motion Pictures.

Abrams, J., Lindelof, D., & Cuse, C. (2004). *Lost*. United States: Bad Robot Productions, Touchstone Television, & ABC Studios.

Silverman, B., Daniels, G., & Gervais, R. (2005). *The Office*. United States: Deedle-Dee Productions, Reveille Productions, & NBC Universal Television Studios.

Seinfeld, J. (2012). *Comedians in Cars Getting Coffee*. United States: Sony Pictures Television.

CPSIA information can be obtained
at www.ICGtesting.com
Printed in the USA
BVHW031307090920
588473BV00001B/17

9 780359 335381